child of nature

Rainmaker Translations supports a series of books meant
to encourage a lively reading experience of contemporary world
literature drawn from diverse languages and cultures. Publication
is assisted by grants from the Black Mountain Institute
(blackmountaininstitute.org) at the University of Nevada,
Las Vegas, an organization dedicated to promoting literary and
cross-cultural dialogue around the world.

child of nature

LULJETA LLESHANAKU

TRANSLATED BY HENRY ISRAELI & SHPRESA QATIPI

A New Directions Book

ACKNOWLEDGMENTS
Some of these poems first appeared in the anthology *Between Water and Song: New Poets
for the Twenty-First Century* (White Pine Press), and in the following journals: *American
Poetry Review, Cerise, Lana Turner, Many Mountains Moving, Per Contra, Pleiades, Quiddity,
Southern Humanities Review, Washington Square, Witness*, and *Words Without Borders*.

   The author would like to thank the Black Mountain Institute at the University of
Nevada, Las Vegas, for a very generous fellowship that allowed her to work on this book.

Author photograph by Mariano Avila

Manufactured in the United States of America
New Directions Books are printed on acid-free paper.
First published as a New Directions Paperbook (NDP 1162) in 2010
Published simultaneously in Canada by Penguin Books Canada Limited

Library of Congress Cataloging-in-Publication Data
Lleshanaku, Luljeta.
 [Fëmijët e natyrës. English]
 Child of nature / Luljeta Lleshanaku; translated from the Albanian by
Henry Israeli and Shpresa Qatipi.
    p. cm.
"A New Directions Book."
ISBN 978-0-8112-1847-4 (pbk.: alk. paper)
 1. Lleshanaku, Luljeta—Translations into English. I. Israeli,
Henry, 1967- II. Qatipi, Shpresa. III. Title.
PG9621.L54F4613 2010
891'.9911—dc22

                                                    2009031746

10 9 8 7 6 5 4 3 2 1

New Directions Books are published for James Laughlin
by New Directions Publishing Corporation
80 Eighth Avenue, New York, NY 10011

For my niece and nephew, Vesa and Gemi Miftari,
to whom I offer this in place of distance

CONTENTS

III

child of nature

I

Darkness has not yet fallen
and from a neighbor's yard
comes a hammer's pounding—
the apiary mended for winter's hibernation.
What good is it knowing who switched off the light?
It's better not to see that face.
Let the last mouthful of light devour itself.
Let the door of the coal stove
enjoy the fading purple glow.
You are old enough
to sit close by with a black poker.
When the room cools down
we both dream of the gypsy woman
the rattling of her silver earrings
her full breasts, and her premonition:
a blue-eyed woman
the birth of six children.

It begins
when she searches in the darkness
for her likeness, a line of verse awaiting its end rhyme
or for a little music, or the exchange of carbon dioxide between
   flowers in the evening
the feeling of turning forty.
And it is just a matter of style
the manner in which she finds herself
because no clashes, no noise at all is expected any longer
the hardest hits already taken
like a statue that's lost its nose.

A forty-year-old woman
is a shadow in search of an object
a voice in the third person, a series of lessons
with little notes written in red, underlined
along the right margin. The space between lines is flesh, is someone
in the waiting room behind a dentist's door
where the stench of arsenic
comes and goes.
Experience, experience, experience!
Little zigzags and a sense of accomplishment
with which the silkworm gnaws the mulberry leaf
starting from the tip.

She makes peace with everything: she keeps her drawers tidy,
practices yoga,
the takeoffs and landings
on the runway of her soul.

When she approaches forty
or better yet, *if* she approaches forty,
because being forty isn't required

it's her choice
like choosing a park bench
that faces away from the street
waiting for no one in particular.

1

Monday feels like an odd shoe
its other chewed by the dog tied at the gate.
The sun always rises through the open backdoor
and pours into the house like birdfeed along the street.
Men returning from the pebble beach
walking with their hands held behind them
on their way to nowhere
look like crosshairs on a gun
their spit still bitter with coffee
dandruff scattered along their collars;
to draw them you would have to hold your breath.
For weeks now there hasn't been a single drop of rain. The thin
                         stream dwindles, sickly, syphilitic.
A child skipping school
sneaks away from his mother.
He is nine and still adds and subtracts on fingers
                 blackened by fresh walnuts
counting the years to his conscription.
He draws a large dusty circle in the dirt
that looks like a piece of blighted flesh
where a tumor had just been removed.

2

Like salmon, ready to mate,
swimming upstream from the sea
to the river's estuary
the wedding guests step backward in time
and beg the landlady to return their flesh:
"Mine is bright white . . ."
"Mine is soft, with a burn from a hot iron on my forearm . . ."
"Mine smells of sage, like a canvas bag . . ."
"Mine is magical, you can wear it inside out . . ."
"Give me anything—it doesn't matter!"

Here comes Mustafa, the drunkard,
with his head stuck to his body's right side.
He is Monday's Saint, guilty of everything,
absorbing everyone's sins
like a swab of alcohol-dabbed cotton
pressed to a wound.

3

Before sleep the world returns whole beneath eyelids
like an army full of pride, gathered under the Arc de Triomphe,
the loot of war behind them.
The nightly rite of fucking
that shredded music
sufficient to hide
the motive for which we woke up this morning
and, even more so, the motive to wake up tomorrow.

The lamp turns off for the last time
and blood continues on its small circular route.

4

When my grandma came here as a bride
with nothing more than her good name
the house was empty but for the hanging weapons.
There was so little here she had to build a whole town
just to find a pair of shoulders for a head.
She began by planting an apricot tree in front of the house
and later another, so that the two were
like hands cupped to a face
to warm it.
Then children dripped from her
as rain from a tin awning.
Those who fell on soft ground were forgotten.
Those on cement
managed to survive.
To this day
they still stand petrified in a black-and-white photograph
in woollen suits with oily unevenly cut hair
looking uncomfortable
looking as if their lives were borrowed from elsewhere.

5

Broken toys were my playthings:
zebras, wind-up Chinese dolls, ice-cream carts
given to me as New Year's presents by my father.
But none was worth keeping whole.
They looked like cakes whose icing had been
                    licked off by a naughty child

until I broke them, cracked and probed their insides, the tiny
                                        gears, the batteries,
not aware then that I was rehearsing
                    my understanding of freedom.

————

When I first looked at a real painting
I took a few steps backward instinctively
                    on my heels
finding the precise place
where I could explore its depth.

It was different with people:
I built them up,
loved them, but stopped short of loving them fully.
None were as tall as the blue ceiling.
As in an unfinished house, there seemed to be a plastic sheet above them
                                        instead of a roof
at the beginning of the rainy autumn of my understanding.

6

Here is the honest man, the just man,
his face a picnic blanket
shaken of crumbs.
His kind never remains unemployed.
He asks, "Does anyone have a nail to drive into
the hole in my chest?"

My great-grandfather was like that,
and so was my grandfather and my father.
Maybe if I were a son I would have been the same,
staring up at a *worthless* father
(What a shame! I'd say).

"How far should I go?" the son would ask only once.
"Until you lose sight of yourself."
It might have been a dream,
because his family tree was struck down by
                              a bolt of lightning
before the succulent scent of burnt sugar emanating from the Katsura
                              spread over the village.

7

The smell of roots in the air, and the rain falling
like bees returning to their hive, all at once.
It's a tradition in my family to distinguish happy rain from melancholy rain
conceived above hilltops during summer.
I listen with one ear, waiting as if for the moment one recognizes that a
   stranger's voice
is indeed one's own voice.

My uncle asks for a "*fazzoletto*" to wipe his glasses.
He has used that word since the time he went to Florence
to have his pneumonia cured—a time he remembers
as fondly as a honeymoon.

With my report card in his hand
veins throb at his temples—a matter of life or death.
He is the one to determine
whether I will be a brick for a wall
or a stone for a barn.
The hand that he hits with
is an instruction manual read only once
although the furrows on his palm—the limits of his destiny—
never leave scars on me.
"To hell with it! Bring me *un fazzoletto*!"

8

"If you have dark skin
your smile is exquisite,
neither incomplete nor flashing rotten teeth."
F. knows this. She mourns for her son.
Early in the morning she opens the window
lights the kerosene stove
with a piece of crumpled telegram still in her hand
sweeps the yard, feeds the chickens, cooks for ten,
fixes the chair with the sphinx's arms
opposite the door.
And each day
with the claws of a hawk she fights against
disorder
begging for form and discipline
like the square plots of a field of wheat
guiding the part of herself that flies mercilessly
in a straight line
never landing.

She accepts greetings with her eyes
and pathways open before her
like the Sabbath among other days,
dedicated to gratitude and prayer.

9

Medio tutissmus ibis, the middle is the safest ground.
The embroidered tablecloth in the middle of the table.
The table in the middle of the carpet.
The carpet in the middle of the room.
The room in the middle of the house.
The house in the middle of the block.
The block in the middle of the town.
The town in the middle of the map.
The map in the middle of the blackboard.
The blackboard in the middle of nowhere.

Lola is an angel. Her forehead hasn't grown since she was eight,
her center of gravity unchanged. And she likes edges, corners,
although she always finds herself
in the middle of the bus
where people rush toward the doors at either end.

My neighbors never went to school
nor have they heard of aesthetics
and hardly ever have they read anything
about the Earth's axes, symmetry, or absolute truth.
But instinctively they let themselves drift toward the middle
like a man laying his head on a woman's lap,
a woman who, with a pair of scissors
will make him more vulnerable than ever
before the day is done.

10

Preparing for winter
isn't tradition, but instinct. We hurl our spare anxieties
like precious cargo from a shipwreck.

Taedium vitae is a time zone
that no longer exists.
The smell of boiled beans separates us
from our neighbors, a dream above the stove
separates us from our ancestors.

There isn't a middleman
between me and my talents.
The wind preaches with the nasal voice of a false prophet.
Years somersault over frozen slopes
and we instinctively hide our heads between our knees.

Limits wither away. My body
more abstract than ever, is a country without an anthem,
a country, delirious and once near death, which I touch
like a mother touching her lips to the forehead of her child
with a high fever.

In my family
prayers were said secretly,
softly, murmured through sore noses
beneath blankets,
a sigh before and a sigh after
thin and sterile as a bandage.

Outside the house
there was only a ladder to climb
a wooden one, leaning against a wall all year long,
ready to use to repair the tiles in August before the rains.
No angels climbed up
and no angels climbed down—
only men suffering from sciatica.

They prayed to catch a glimpse of Him
hoping to renegotiate their contracts
or to postpone their deadlines.

"Lord, give me strength," they said
for they were descendants of Esau
and had to make do with the only blessing
left over from Jacob,
the blessing of the sword.

In my house praying was considered a weakness
like making love.
And like making love
it was followed by the long
cold night of the body.

Large, grey, sprawled
like an old elephant.
Winter is ending.
Low, sloping roofs are overturned boats
slumbering along the shores of drowsiness.

Twenty years of an oak tree's life
burns instantly in a stove.
And eyes meet only by accident
suburban roads
that intersect in grassy meadows
streams that swell their banks
hairs on a pillow
after a long illness.

The old elephant's hoof
tramples the ground
sewing poisonous yellow flowers
in its path
flowers without scent.

In times without truth there are no taboos.
Maybe this yellow book is one of a few that survived
although the act of hiding it
lives on in our minds.

In the scorching heat, dinner is served clumsily every night
at the same hour, the hour when light and dark cover us equally.
Something is quickly cooked; a calf's head perhaps, of which I'll
    get the tongue.
They say that if you eat it your tongue will grow
and if you eat the eyes you will be a sharpshooter
and if you eat books you will eat yourself
little by little, from the edges to the center,
like tractors harvesting at collective farms.

From the head of the table, the head of the family
fingers his warts while lecturing on evolution:
"The strongest die, the weakest survive."

Nothing distinguishes this from a holy dinner
where food and wine are portioned out equally—
only the truth is read secretly
by the mystified, sharing it
like a yellow book.*

* *Yellow books were books banned under the Communist regime.*

In the country, fate steps
softly, never rushes anywhere
traverses the crucifixes
of cart tracks in the dirt.

A chimney exhales rings of smoke
and the sky's black fingers twirl them
across the blind milky way.

Through the iron bars
of a little pub window
light spills out in white rectangles
like playing cards
overturned on a dusty table.

The night watchman's dog
sits on a rickety chair
wagging its tail,
drooling, belching at stars.

And the shingle-covered roofs
clustered together in groups of four or five
resemble the scaly backs of crocodiles
drifting downriver
making sounds
not unlike drowning men.

In the village nestled between two mountains
the news always arrives one month late,
cleansed in transit, glorified, mentioning only the dead who made
    it to paradise,
and a coup d'etat referred to as "God's will."

Spring kills solitude with solitude, imagination
the sap that shields you from your body. Chestnut trees
awaken, drunken men
lean their cold shoulders against a wall.

The girls here always marry outsiders and move away
leaving untouched statues of their fifteen-year-old
selves behind.

But the boys bring in wives
from distant villages,
wives who go into labor on heaps of grass and straw in a barn
and bear prophets.
Forgive me, I'd meant to say "only one will be a prophet."
The others will spend their lives throwing stones
(that is part of the prophesy, too).

At noon on an autumn day like today
they will bolt out of school like a murder of crows stirred by the
    smell of blood
and chase the postman's skeleton of a car
as it disappears around a corner, leaving only dust.

Then they will steal wild pears from the "bitch's yard"
and nobody will stop them. After all, she deserves it. She's sleeping
    with two men.

Between the pears in one boy's schoolbag
lies a copy of *Anna Karenina*.
It will be skimmed over, impatiently, starting on the last page
cleansed and glorified, like old news.

No need to fill in a form
or to tap your fingertips with annoyance.

No need to do anything
in a place run by ghosts—
the temple stones lugged from afar, perhaps as far as a kilometer—
to taste the geometry of shadows.

The doors are open because there's nothing to steal
from the city-state of diseased poets.
Like bandages on scuffed eyebrows
the postboxes open only when wet.

A town without advertisements, without pretty women
selling cavity-free smiles, without streets pointing to the suburbs,
the limits of cognition—the dictatorship of a blade of grass.

I greet my neighbors, but they don't return the favor.
What's the point of wishing someone good luck
when one is born and dies in a single day, perhaps within an hour?

Here they all are! On my worktable,
on the backs of books, little photos,
with the garden of Eden gleaming in the background,
stuck like receipts to the neatly hung clothes at the drycleaner's.

And finally, astonishingly, I don't know how to name this place.
A nation without martyrs doesn't have a name.
Deserters, yes, are branded, as Spartan deserters once were,
with half-shaved faces—
light and darkness come together.

Don't blame me for losing the ability to see what's near.
A bay with no harbor,
I grew up without being kissed on the forehead at bedtime.
I never heard cryptic footsteps beneath my window
and no one whispered in my ear.
The olive grove in my yard was state owned
and looked like armor riddled by bullets; even after a bumper crop
not a single olive reached our table.
Never has a glass, bearing the impression of my lips,
shattered. Maybe it was because of superstition
but dishes were washed instantly, and never broke.
Never have I rummaged through a drawer
that didn't give a slapped puppy yelp.
And never have I seen the flickering of a nightdress
gliding stealthily between rooms
nor felt the warmth of things that were solely mine—
the banister that led to my floor of dreams—
things belonging to me and things I belonged to.
My strength never came from the inside
but from the outside,
smoked meat
at the mercy of salt and frost.

Never have I savored the sweet taste of blame
nor the tartness of repentance
portioned out like halvah
at a requiem.

I'm waiting for a poem,
something rough, not elaborate or out of control,
something undisturbed by curses, a white raven
released from darkness.

Words that come naturally, without aiming at anything,
a bullet without a target,
warning shots to the sky
in newly occupied lands.

A poem that will well up in my chest

and until it arrives
I will listen to my children fighting in the next room
and cast my gaze down at the table
at an empty glass of milk
with a trace of white along its rim
my throat wrapped in silver
a napkin in a napkin ring
waiting for late guests to arrive. . . .

My daughter laughs at how I choose which clothes to wear
at how I keep my hair pinned to one side
like a little girl in white stockings
waiting anxiously for someone
to push her swing.
Others laugh at how I walk
or sleep on my stomach, or eat with one hand. . . .
I too laughed at my mother
when she came to the parent-teacher conference
with her hair still wet
coffee stains on the corners of her lips
her dumpy clothes, thick gnarled stockings,
an old-fashioned necklace with an amulet
turned yellow from sunlight.

And today, here we are, she and I, like two sides of the same yard—
one in the front, the other in the rear.
We seek attention differently, she and I:
she like a dervish sticking pins under her skin
and I
crumpling the wrapper of a chocolate.

Among seven days, eight are faded out
like the armpits and chests of denim work clothes.
You're one of us!

Among seven women, eight have swollen varicose veins
and kidneys wrapped tight with woolen sashes.
You're one of us!

The youngest imitates her mother's pain, hands on waist
trying to gain her acceptance.
You're one of us!

Flitting around, with an egg in her mouth, shouting her dreams
then crushing them with stones, like dwindling fires lit by children.
You're one of us!

Either scorn or be scorned
if you are a seed that doesn't lay roots.
But when I produced scorn like a penknife out of my pocket
it failed to cut:
"Watch out! You'll cut your hands! Put that thing away!"
You're one of us!

Homonymic lives, all of ours,
mine no exception
misery that old typewriter
with its accent key missing.
You're one of us!

Me, one of them
and in two places simultaneously.
I, the premonition of another life.

Nonsense! Why would you wait for something created out of
   nothing?
Despite the washed and pressed sheets
the sterilized scalpel, iodine, the basket of biological vowels
and the nightshift doctor napping on a chair
like a landlady waiting for her husband
to come back empty-handed from hunting,
my autogenetically born child still wails.
My body, as if aimed by catapult at a disinfectant-sprayed wall
finds it difficult to be indoors
to awaken the distaste of three generations
and its only motive is continuity, hostage taking, and a political cause
tricky as the screech of a night owl that awakens an avalanche.
A window slams shut; tobacco gardens bend
in awe toward the soul that first shaped despair.
Now comes more crying.
Behold which grandmother or great-grandmother of mine fell into
   that trap
which one chose my daughter's body
as a witness: what she saw, heard, or touched
and more importantly, what she thought—but a witness isn't
   allowed to think
after swearing herself in on the battered book of truth
with an illiterate hand.

Not always does the plague of the first born
pass over the doorway architrave
smeared with blood.

Does the powerful and irreversible tempest drive away
those who believe they are destined for the Promised Land?
And does it divide them along the way?

I remember when I was ten
my happy, restless wanderings,
a spoon beating white merangue.

I felt my soul radiating
from my warm body,
fragrance from blossoming night flowers.

That wasn't freedom. Freedom wasn't a feeling of spaciousness.
Freedom was a vertical ascension
sacks of sand hauled by hot air balloons—
a sacred suspension!

I shake these memories from my body
as a zealot would shake dust from a carpet
whose arabesque wakes him from a dreamy sleep.

At last I am free from the illusion of freedom.
Now I am free.

Prisoners
guilty or not
always look the same when they are released—
patriarchs dethroned.

This one just passed through the gate
head bowed despite not being tall
his gestures like a Bedouin's
entering the tent
he carried on his back all day long.

Cotton curtains, stone walls, the smell of burnt lime
take him back to the moment
the cold war ended.

The other day his sheet was hung up in the courtyard
as if to flaunt the blood stain
after a wedding night.

Faces tarnished by sun
surround him, all eyes and ears:
"What did you dream of last night?"
A prisoner's dreams
are parchment
made sacred by its missing passages.

His sister is still discovering his odd habits:
the bits of bread hidden in pockets and under his bed
the relentless chopping of wood for winter.

Why this fear?
What can be worse than life in prison?

Having choices
but being unable to choose.

They are dying one after the other;
shoveling earth on them has become as common
as sprinkling salt on food.

They all are of the same generation, my family,
or more accurately, of one era,
and the children of an era are like dogs tied to a sled:
in their search for gold
they either run together or fall together.

It is not mathematics,
but more like combs, combs which tame any hair's rebellion
after a mad flirtation before a mirror.

The words we speak do not tell linear stories—
they are our living fossils.
Cats, unlike us, are all instinct,
their escape routes written in black-and-white
in arrows, crosses, and dashes.

Some say the morning birds, not cats or dogs, absorb
the whole day's warmth. I absorb the energy
of people close to me
as cats do.
A pure energy
with no electrons to exchange
the energy of an ice cube dazzling in a glass–
the energy of people thinking aloud
exchanging ideas.

My people do everything loudly.
They suffer loudly; even their silence is loud.
Their fruit always ripens too soon.

It's not heroism when at night, in secret,
the muezzin chanted verses of the Koran to us
and I lost my connection to everyone around me.
It was as if they stopped thinking
and dozed off, elbow to elbow,
like a vineyard after the harvest
no longer needing to be protected.

II

CHESS

Autumn. Veins of marble
swell in the rain.

The graves of my relatives
four inches of space between them
lined up
like cars at a railroad crossing.

What once kept them together
like fingers in an ironsmith's glove
has vanished. . . . The war is over.

In the afterlife there are only a few strangers
waiting for the train to pass. . . .

The smell of the earth
reminds me of home
where a clock that once hung on the wall is missing.

I polish the dust off their names with care—
the years . . . like little bruises on a knee,
love . . . which now pricks less
than the thorns of a rose.

There, at the entrance to the cemetery
the guard sits in his booth
playing chess with himself.

My portrait hasn't changed much.
My head still leans a little to one side
in the same way
as if asking for an apology.
Apology? For what?
Because I was in the wrong place at the right time,
or in the right place at the wrong time,
or both? Because I was present
when asked to be invisible?
Asked not to tap a spoon against my teeth while eating, not to dream
  out loud,
not to make smoke when I get burned, not to make suds when I wash,
asked to remove my feathers when I crumble
when the elastic breaks and my soul lands between my feet
asked not to bother fixing it?
And believe me, life is light when you are invisible.
I followed the path I was told to follow.
Glass! First I was glass, full of curses, the elementary school's window
made visible by dust.
Then I was the glass of a monocle that one eye trusted and the other didn't.
Later, after I began to write, I became the thick glass
of a telescope
that revealed stars on the palm of a hand.
The eyes that peer through me still look tired,
and the stars, still millions of light years away.
I bear no false news, only a premonition;
my deception has distance.

Maybe someday, I won't be an invisible thing,
a winding border between two worlds.
I will have a voice, a color, and be read on rainy days
well aware that a timid nod to a photographer
is merely an alibi.

It enters my days arrogantly
like the silence after the clap
of a judge's mallet.

I sway in the slightest breeze
across a field of wheat
awaiting the harvest.

It arrives when I think I'm safe
when I think all I am is just a spine,
strong, without a chest or a belly,
without a navel—
like a cellar full of food
stored for winter.

I hesitate for a second
ready to start over again
with a clean painter's palette
dark fingerprint in its center.

Then I set off on the same road
the end of which I know best:
a cold bullet bulging in my pocket
the one every good soldier saves
for the day he finds himself surrounded.

Irreversible is the river
on whose back
dead leaves swirl.
Irreversible are words—
the dust of roads
mingled with breath, warm breath
that sticks to our trembling lips
like fog to a boat.

Irreversible is this cup of tea
irreversible the restrained aura of melancholy
after a superficial conversation
about books and cemeteries.
Perhaps even routine—
the eggcup
that keeps half of our round selves
in balance—
is irreversible.

Irreversible are all moments of love
even when they happen more and more frequently
even when skin turns to moss.
In love two bodies become one cactus
fused always
to that instant of death.

In the morning, particularly in the morning,
my body stretches out, each part distinct, formless,
like a gun dismantled on a tablecloth.

Yesterday is volcanic stone
perfection itself
nothing to add or remove.

And then there's him, lying on his side,
clay that can be shaped in endless ways.
"Is it time for coffee?"

And although he is still sleeping
with the face of a stranger, the face of sleep,
a face without memory,
it is he and only he who knows my body's code
that flows like a river by a colony of gypsies
unaware of its source or estuary.

My head on your left shoulder
is a zero valence—a grey metallic loneliness.
Freckles, spots of rust . . .
Time drips slowly, mercury in the thermometer
hung on the wall shyly slides away
—autumn's striptease
revealing what was hidden.

Each night, the same nightmare.
The silkworm
gnaws at fresh leaves
and your shadow slips from the chair
like a low-cut evening dress
I once wore.

Your zero valence is
a hopeless chemical loneliness—
burning flesh,
black suffocating gases.

Unconditional love
has always frightened me—
as has the stewardess in white, there, near the exit
who directs us to fasten our seatbelts
near the end of the journey.

THE ISLAND

You and I
live on an island
far from cities with traffic lights and people.

Outside we hear the rustlings
of a bed of reeds
where the wind with its toothless mouth blows
luring in tides.

A boat is moored on the shore
a forlorn boat
rotting in the rain.

It seems
we'll never be able to use it
to sail home.

That was it.
Now body, breath, and tree are one.
Tree? What tree? There's no tree beyond the window
no tree to crave
the tranquility of bodies washed ashore.

A little courage is all I need
to open my eyes and confront
the fearful scene before me—
the moon at midday
coming into focus in the dome of the sky.

Sometimes my belly contracts
like a cobra
that just swallowed its prey.
Yours rises and falls, without pause, never understated,
inclusive as a manifesto.

Nothing could change that rhythm.
There will be little mute cracks in porcelain
dessert knives
routine things
and when wind takes shape
the death of imagination.

What tree?

Now our breathing is steady
grammatical
blades of grass and mud
in a nest recently abandoned.

We smile a little
like a pair of sandals
that expose no toes or heels
resting at the foot of a tree.

All that has happened is
someone's conscience
has gone haywire:
our past three years, collected
in the pages of a diary,
lie scattered beneath cliffs.

Our silhouettes on the bed
look like a pair of scissors
left wide open
rusted bolt at its center.

Your breathing: thin, quiet.
Mine: dense, troubled.
Dispersed unevenly
we are like crumbs
cast off after a rushed meal.

Lulling in the curiosity of an evening movie
the four of us look like pieces broken off a relic,
small and large fragments
caught in an archaeologist's sieve.

Ribs, elbows, shoulders, and knees
lean freely against one another.
The illusion, flickering, reflects
off the screen onto the ionic architecture of our flesh.

"We might have been happy," you utter
with the same compassionate tone
you use when talking about the dog tied to a pole in the courtyard
on that fearful night of lightning.
We turn out the lights, get ready for bed,
our heads glowing like lemons in the dark,
sour and dissatisfied.

"We could . . . if . . ."

We hide beneath a suffocating embrace
simply to avoid speaking
simply because we fear that we might have to tell a story
a story whose ending we don't yet know
because we no longer hear barking in the courtyard.

Clay turns on its wheel
unable to realize
that it is history itself
that same story
told over and over in countless ways.

When the limit of what you know runs circles around you
like the bubble in the compass of a little fishing schooner
that returns to the same shore each night
and you breathe in philosophy like incense
just accept it. The moment your life is replaced
with another is here—
your soul exchanged for that of a jackal
or a shark in open seas, or a butterfly balanced above an elephant's eye
or a lumberjack walking three hours
to get to the nearest pub.
At least now I know why you were always
so late.

But I'll never speak a word of thanks
for you who protected me from the unmistakable underbelly of things
feeling cold and tedious as a helmet.

Evening. Two or three taxis line up in a row
waiting for someone who's lost.

The room, just as I left it this morning
only the sheets have been changed
by hands I have never known
only the rain taps lightly against the window
like a withered bouquet of flowers.

The message on the answering machine is still there
the voice of a man
looking for a woman who slept here months earlier
a woman who had wiped herself dry with these same towels
clean and perfumed.

I replay it several times
piece together their past
try to avoid the question: "What might have happened next?"

A telephone call from a phone booth
and then he arrives hurriedly and, perhaps, with great longing.
His lips wipe makeup off my face
carelessly and without pause
as the understudy does after the show.

Finally, I lie down on the bed
made by anonymous hands
stretching out among my lost words
(anxious, hurried questioning)
like a silk bookmark
between newly read pages of a book.

Like eels reaching the sea
or elephants returning to the smooth humus of riverbanks
we embark on a long journey
to decide where to bury you.

When I die, which door
will be slammed loudest by the stormy wind?
There is no death between need and excess.
Our last bed will be but a pair of eyes.
The soul, the last to go,
separates the walnut tree
from its shadow.

Look how deeply you sleep!
The sleep of an infant
ill-fitted for old age . . .

The spectacles placed crosswise by the bed
are waiting for someone's breath to fog them.
Beyond their rims objects are magnified, palpable,
clear, and raw
as on the world's first day.

I am a heavy and lazy beast
digging up soil with my nails.
And if this is my last resting place
then I will never hear a twig break
hundreds of kilometers away.
The magnificent rituals of the forest in winter will continue
with an ice-cold heart
with a heart of snow.

The city has expanded
a diaphragm heaving open
a single bus stop now separating it from the cemetery.

There, seated on a stool, waits a widow, money
for a ticket clenched in her fist.
At home she cleaned herself up to her shoulders with alcohol
her body free of cuts and scratches.

Getting off the bus, she fixes her gaze on its license plate.
Her breasts, like flowers, droop
as soft rain falls like apostrophes
in a conversation between two worlds.

In winter, no one is at the bus stop
but the driver waits there habitually, the engine idling,
half a cigarette
dampened between his lips.
Soon the automatic door closes, springing back in place
like the last words of a verdict.

No one knows which expanded first,
the city or cemetery, a tango
with arms extended and thighs drawn up—
currents in open water.

Two people form a habit.
Three people make a story.

A dog digs through the wedding trash:
Champagne bottles, cake, filets of beef, caviar,
a butchery of vows made in one night.

A castle would simply be called a "palace"
if it weren't for the barbarian assault.

The echoes of obstacles are heard:
someone who protects you from forgetfulness,
his pain petrified.

They remember nights on the soft grave
of an anonymous Turkish soldier, making love.
His hairy shoulder was a fig leaf
trying to touch the reptilian sky
that tomorrow would slide over everyone
like a bar of soap in a public restroom.
She had freckles; he had strong instincts.
That was enough reason for them to meet again and again
without setting a fixed time.
And perhaps, he could catch that piece of sky
if she weren't so alarmed:
"Nobody's here! I want to go home!"

There is no third eye,
no self-destructive gene
to stop freedom from growing without intention
like the cancerous cells of a tumor.

The third eye will accommodate them
inside a frame, an apple bitten from both sides in their hands.
Aging starts now.

That night, when they returned, they were only two,
less than one,
shaking off blades of grass from their bodies,
metastases of an everlasting summer.

It always happens in the late afternoon
when the damp air stinks of oblivion
and the procession makes its way
toward a safe corner of town
like a caterpillar having just crawled
from a crack in the wall.

From a distance, women's knees flash
between skirts and stockings,
plump knees uncared for
like winter apples split in half.

And men lean their arms against the coffin
ever so gently
with no more effort
than it takes to nudge an old pot across the floor
to catch a leak.

With their free arms
they pluck oak leaves from their black suits,
clothes worn only for weddings and funerals.
And later that evening, they clean the dust and grey hairs off
with a brush and drops of vinegar
(although they may never be worn again).
And their shoes grow used to
the deafness of mud
along cemetery lanes.

I try to guess
what remains after a small town funeral.
Maybe nothing.
Not much pain, not much forewarning.

Not even wild roses or rosemary.
Only ghosts and oak leaves
humbly accepting
the gift of the first raindrops.

The snow comes late this year. Violet shadows
doze like shepherds around
a white fire.
The swaying shadow of a fence looks like a woman's clavicle—
a woman who dreams of her lover's journey home through the snow,
his late return.

Thin trails lead to the doorway.
A car parked for hours
compresses black earth.
Radio signals float out of earshot.
A boat with its eel fishers
in luminous raincoats skims by.
A child—his little hands trembling—
casts slanting trees across the table.

The choir kneels.
The moment has come to speak
in a voice I have never known before.

I raise my head and see a single star in the night sky
shapeless and fearful like the shard of a broken bottleneck,
a star I have for years foolishly followed.
Perhaps the shadow of my infinite persistence
looks like a large hill
on the moon, a camel bent over a puddle
preparing for a new stretch of thirst.

The peak, covered in snow
all year long,
reflects the sky, but like a dogma
never touches it.

The electrocardiogram of sweat dried in the body
spreads from shirt to shirt
contagious as a flame, infecting everyone with its slow rhythm
to the youngest in the family, a little boy
lingering like a postscript
to everything that's already been said.

But it's not hard work that sweetens the cabbage,
harvests the corn, or repairs the beehives.

It's that warm sigh, while staring at the mountain
on the other side of which
"life is, of course, better."

The sigh is like a woman who sleeps with everybody.
Do whatever you want to her
but never ask her name
even as you leave.

Everyone here resembles each one another,
not because of incest, but because they all fuck
the same woman
who emits pheromones of the Unknown.

The Centaur constellation
highlights a narrow goat's path,
the only way out of the village.
"Good-bye," is often heard, but never "Welcome!"

The doors, decorated with mignonettes,
are a euphemism for the fear
that one day someone will return
to tell of what happens on the other side of the mountain.

III

No one noticed me
at my parents' wedding—
my face scrunched
as if I had eaten sour fruit—
tucked away like a wet invitation in a pocket.

Soon thereafter,
my mother swung the window of her chest shut
and opened a larger one on her belly
overlooking the street
in the morning
as the scent of fresh coffee
and toast wafted in.

She knew what she desired.
I was her pure, perfect objective,
I, who humbly flew from her body—
a magpie with a diamond in its throat
a novel read aloud, beginning on the last page.

The newly opened jars of cream
in her dresser drawers
were out of bounds for me
as were the untouched perfumes and powders
lipstick the size of a finger
pointing seductively to exotic places.

I was there until the very moment
chromosomes were combined—
a handful of hazelnuts with a handful of ginger—
but not a moment later.

Waking is an obligation:
three generations open their eyes every morning
inside me.

The first is an old child—my father;
he always chooses his luck and clothes one size too small for him.

Next comes grandfather . . . In his day, the word "diagnosis" did not exist.
He simply died of misery six months after his wife.
No time was wasted. Above their corpses
rose a factory to make uniforms for dockworkers.

And great-grandfather, if he ever existed,
I don't even know his name. Here my memory goes on hiatus,
my peasant origins cut like the thick and yellow nails
of field-workers.

Three shadows loom like a forest over me
telling me what to do
and what not to do.

You listened to me say "good morning"
but it was either an elephant pounding on a piano
or the seams coming apart in my father's little jacket.

Indeed, my father, his father, and his father before that
are not trying to change anything
nor do they refuse to change anything; the soap of ephemerality
leaves them feeling fresh and clean.

They only wish to gently touch the world again
through me, the way latex gloves
lovingly touch the evidence
of a crime scene.

MEN

Human existence is like a dead language
of which only an expression, a quotation, or a single word remains.

But a man without sons is a mutation.
His name will move from one ear to another by a clean female whisper
voiced like a dream without conflict
difficult to remember after night's end.

Six daughters, each birth a failure
like the gold prospector
who brings home only silk and medicinal herbs.

Without a son in the family,
there is no river to carry the toxic remains
of his black-and-white anger,
no one to foresee war in the bones of the pet
sacrificed for dinner;
no wars, no births or deaths
when life gets lazy in peacetime.

His cell is a cave
sketched with naive carbon drawings:
the hunter against the beast, the hunter against nature,
until the moment a woman appears around the fire.
Then strength moves from his muscles
to his eyes.
and the angle of the arrow's aim shifts.

This is the end of the ice age
the end of clarity.

There is a secret that extinguishes men from the inside
like Dwarf Stars
changing from yellow to white
and then . . . to black, a smudge across the cosmos.
There is no son to inherit the father's secret. . . .
not the secret itself
but the art of solitude.

In the sweltering August of 1972
the napes of the movers' necks look green
as they load furniture onto a truck.
"Watch out! Don't step on the flowers!" my mother warns.
The flowers would whither three days later. . . .
The house empties out as if by x-ray
and the neighbors' compassion
melts away, an ice compress
held against a wound.

We move somewhere else,
where gratitude instills itself like balconies on faces
and adventure is fixed on a stick
like a rooster-shaped lollipop.

I am only three. I do not know what promises are
and no one tells me
that a childhood without promises is bread
without yeast, still sweet yet tough and dry.

My father cannot be seen anywhere
for my father has not yet been born.
He will be born in another chapter
much later
when I begin to feel the need to be someone's protector
a little shadow growing slowly between my legs
like a microphone stand.

In the heart of November, the cold wind blowing
as at the end of days,
snow and my mother's face
wait in the backseat to test out
their philosophy of inevitability.
Lightbulbs, like a row of ants, lead
to the dining room. I am the bride
at the end of the ceremony. And when I get ready to sleep,
carefully removing twenty-one pins from my hair,
as many as the years behind me,
I barely know anything about life
but I do know that when turning a corner
even headlights are worthless.

I try to hide my happiness,
an orange dressed in white fuzz.
I emerge cunningly from my genetic prophecy
as one leaves a cave eroded by loneliness
hidden inside the largest ram's belly.

If I attempt to draw the curtain a little
with two well-manicured fingertips
two shadows will pass by in harmony on the black asphalt,
the musician and the cello after the concert—
the man and the woman who defied predictability.

Shaving *after* work? What for?
It reminds me of my father
a long time ago
standing before a mirror, cracked as
corn grits cooked without fat.
He went on shaving at that hour
a razor sliding up and down
clearing a path from temple to chin
like the words of an apostle
and as his tongue twisted like a snail
emptying one cheek and filling the other
his words rebounded from the glass:
"The power of a man, my son,
is measured by the things he doesn't do.
Passion should be kept hidden, like a turnip!"

It was as if breaking a rule, almost blasphemy
when I, years later,
early in the morning, before doing any housework
started shaving my own "thorn bush"
using my father's razor.

When my hand trembled, I called out to God.
It wasn't difficult. It was like searching for a barber
in a familiar neighborhood.
God is not used to saying, "What can I do for you, young man?"
The cross is older than man.

Here I am, without a single cut
my neck lit up as if by an internal lamp.
"A clean shave," my dad always said,
my dad whose eyes at death—

his face unshaven for days
looking like a swarm of ants
trying to lift a grain of wheat—
caved in like the crumpled napkin of a child
made to leave the table
still hungry.

A LIST OF THINGS TO DO

I always promise to come see you
but I never keep my promises
when they have anything to do with you

when you are just a name
on my list of things to do
always something more pressing
because you will always wait. . . .

There's always a winter not far behind. . . .
How difficult it must have been for you
without a glass of warm tea in the evening
tortured between cold walls
like quicksilver in mortar
now used to fill teeth.

There's always an early summer. . . .
with the sound of your neighbor and his son
who at the strike of midnight
always come home quarrelling

while you hold a photo of a girl, cut out of the newspaper,
the atrophied song of grasshoppers in the background
chirping away until noon the next day.

Sometimes when you were no longer here
I would draw a long line across
your name on my list
beginning from the left, straight through to the right,
like the holy commandments written in the Koran
no possibility
of turning back,
father.

It's Sunday. On the soles of shoes
walking in the hallway
snow turns to plasma, and the memories of roads disappear.

A 150-watt lamp in the middle of the room
looks like a piece of yellow cheese caught in a trap of boredom.
My mother knits, quietly counting stitches—
she always knows how many are needed, even when swapping rows.
She is stuck to her seat like putty in the corner of a window
becoming more and more clearly defined over the years.
She is a pin cushion.
She knows the art of submission instinctively
and tries to teach it to me
and my sister.
We are three Matrioshka dolls lined up by size.
I am the last one—
the one that doesn't pull apart.

Just when I'm about to share
the discomfort of a long journey
with someone else's eyes
I notice my mother
carefully following the stewardess
perform the safety instructions
between first class and coach.

The skin on her jaw stiffens
as she prays to her gods.

I try to understand the years that divide
the woman of my childhood from the one here today.
My mother never believed in miracles.
She would unwittingly crush the north star
with a flap of the blinds
for fear her children would catch cold.
She believed only in her touch
the rough horizontal knowledge
of two hands swollen by lye and water.

I am thinking,
How many digressions, from childhood to today,
separate me
from this little marionette, so easily manipulated,

when she reaches her right hand beneath her seat
to touch the orange life jacket
like a child touching a book of fairy tales under her bed.

My deskmate in elementary school
had blue nails, blue lips, and a big irreparable hole in his heart.
He was marked by death. He was invisible.
He used to sit on a stone
guarding our coats
as we played in the playground, that alchemy of sweat and dust.

The one marked to be king
is cold, ready for a free fall
born prematurely from a sad womb.

And the redheaded woman waiting for her drunk husband to return
will go on waiting for one hundred years.
It isn't the alcohol; she is marked by "waiting."
And he only as guilty as an onlooker
pushed indoors by rain.

What's more, it isn't the war
that took the life of the young boy
with melancholy eyes. He was marked as well, born to be on the
 recruiter's list.
Melancholy is the standard arsenal of war.

And then there is one marked for survival
who will continue to eat his offspring like a polar bear
that never notices the warming climate.

All of them are as closed as theorems, their sky
a rental home
where hammering even a single nail of change is forbidden.

They are waiting for their next command, which they will ignore anyway
like the Argonauts who filled their ears with wax
and rowed on through the sirens' path.

I am a man without land.
Everything I have is written diagonally across my face,
the word "fragile" on a gift sent
during the holidays.

My grandfather grappled with his land
like a wolf in a trap
all alone in the world.

It was a fight without surprises, with intermittent ceasefires
and without flesh wounds: it was all-consuming.

His steps were enormous, his gaze like the mouth of a flesh-eating
   plant
empty and free of assumptions.

When he lost the fight
he turned around and saw
all that had happened behind him:
the manna tree grew tall, overshadowing the neighbor's yard,
his wife dead with one foot bare
and his sons aged into old bachelors.

My grandfather never built a tower. Instead, he spoke a horizontal
   language
and talked to God through it: he bought land, a lot of land. He
   bought continuity
and he swore at his creator who once told him
that he would never be able to think about tomorrow.

I am different; I am a man without land
and nothing ever happens behind my back.
I always live in the moment
like a wet piece of paper
stuck to the bumper of a truck traveling down the road.

It's midnight, and a worker returning
from the second shift at the cannery
tests what strength he has left

by throwing stones against the tiles
of the madwoman's roof.

"Damn you all, you sons of bitches!"
she curses from inside.

She is history, unable to cast blame on anyone.
She is the skeleton key, the collective curse
on a night that reeks of sardines and enzymes.

His roof more red than the others, and above it
the television antenna
vibrating like a shrub on the edge of a cliff—
the only one among fifty houses.

They called him "the orphan" when he was a child
and the nickname stuck
and grew like a scar along his body.

He built his house by himself and then bought a television;
wolves attack the throat
where prey is most vulnerable.

His gate stands wide open in the evenings,
an orgy of shoes in the corridor.
"Goal!" and "Ah!" crystallize in the air,
and his elbows tuck in during sad movies.

He never forgets a bone for his dog
and the coffee is always freshly brewed.

They call him "the television's owner" now,
a nickname he likes. More than anyone he knows
his identity is not a question of a proper noun, but of a possessive.

He admires visitors
while they admire his blue tube.
Each envies the other. A chain.
A caravan drawn to an oasis
in the dunes.

When his wife died
he married her sister
to buy himself some time.

Fat, childish, obsessed with cleaning
a muzzle-loading musket
she never complained. With gold earrings
and bruises he planted on her face
she had all the solemnity of a married woman.

He gave her a small plot
and she built a colony.
She gave him many children
who grew up close to the earth—
strawberries with round eyes and thorns—
shooing geese from a zone of amnesty
with gnarled sticks in their hands.

In what seemed a few minutes
his world moved from the front door
to the back stairs.

Now, exhausted, she snores with her mouth wide open
against a pillow, a supporting wall
between him and his consciousness.

Both find ways to lie to themselves:
he asking her to resist him more
and she—like the houses along the border
where the pleasure of contraband
has replaced cards on birthdays.

THE CINEMA

Without fail
Sundays at the cinema
were always rainy days
big black umbrellas
clashing against the ticket booth.

The doorman among the torn stubs
looked like a watercolor
hung crookedly on a kitchen wall.
We waited anxiously in the front row
looking straight ahead and
eating sunflower seeds
toasted over the ashes of textbooks
until the horizontal beam lit
a band of white dust and settled on the screen
and halos lit up over our heads—
a holy family in a Byzantine painting.

Always the same old films
soundtrack crackling like handfuls of rice
thrown at the newlyweds' white car.
Beautiful actors kissed
as if for the first time.

When the lights came on
and we saw our faces
and shook out our frozen limbs
we were an allegory for desire and disappointment
pale fences in our backyards
on which mother used to dry the laundry—
fences that were once full of color and life.

B talks about the afterlife
with the same degree of certainty
as a farmer who hangs his work clothes
behind the door late in the evening.

This is not a joke. . . .

For years he followed the parallel lines
his paralyzed father's wheelchair made,
lines, which looped into large knots
like shoelaces tied impatiently.
Years later, when his wife left him—
he recalls it was summer—
he went to the garden as usual
gathered the rotten fruit fallen at night
to avoid attracting wasps
and closed the door behind her
faintly, without anger,
the way he used to fasten the buttons
on the back of her evening dress.
The next morning, when he had breakfast, he tasted
each morsel
with gratitude
a toothless chewing
like believers seated in the front row
of church on Sunday, muttering psalms.

The children he never had
continue coming home late at night,
sweaty, filthy, and with lame excuses
on the tips of their tongues.
He listens to them
while clipping his nails, and hesitates,

a fetus preparing for birth.

History always happens somewhere else,
and like a railway keeper
clearing the sleepers of weeds and stones
or tightening a loose screw

he does not see it, but knows of power,
knows better than anyone when to get off the track
while listening with one ear against a rail.

THE SMELL OF MILK

in memory of H. Kupi

Now
after many, many years
I can probably ask myself
how I was related to that old
cherry tree trunk of a man.

We shared plenty of time together. . . .
When he would recount his dreams of the previous night
he moved his hands,
shovels clearing streets of snow.
He would read pages of his diary
written during the heat of the day
anticipating every comma, every word, every pause
with his forefinger,
the finger of fate, getting ahead of itself.

We would speak in English
an archaic dialect learned in prisons.
He would search out the translation
for Albanian words
trying to pronounce them with
desperate, faintly audible sounds,
grey hair stuck in a comb.

He taught me to ask "How are you?"
while looking directly into the other's eyes.

On the mantelpiece
the photos of women in the family
alive or dead, all bent at the edges.
Their bellies, crossed by their hands
were houses nailed shut during epidemics.

It was the same every day.
Hours followed hours
until I grew impatient
or the sheep's milk would overflow into the fire.

Only later, when there were no longer diaries,
when the cherry tree was gone, when the chimney crumbled,
when the photographs faded into silence
could I smell the piercing odor of burning milk
and know that these days were coming to an end.

I was no longer a child
a child with whom the testament of reading could be trusted

. . . speaking to a child
is like trampling on fallen leaves
never waiting to be asked "why" or "how."

I am searching for a way to come back
something I have never been able to do before
without chipping off even a single grain from the statue of salt
a statue always facing away from me.

I will make no more promises
I will no longer believe in the pretty house
with an idyllic cloud hovering above it.

I will choose the same route, the same path I took that day I fled
following claw marks left by a bear
on tree trunks it could not climb.

I will return to pick up where history left off
like lightning
striking a furrowed field.

I will return,
simply, without time to rationalize it
like when searching for the eyes on a tight-fitting mask
or when winter approaches, smothering all fear beneath it,
a time of awakening.

A few years ago I was invited to spend a few months at an artists' colony in New Hampshire. While I was there I wrote several poems, but after I gained some distance from the work, I threw out almost all of them. I felt as if I was following the wrong star, as if I had falsely adapted my literary sensibilities to an American aesthetic. It was too easy to embrace the philosophy of a culture immersed in a long tradition of individualism, metaphysical perspectives, and continuity, where artists and writers simply add a stone in a wall that has been under construction for centuries. It is a philosophy completely alien to my culture.

In Albania everything happens in twenty-four hours. Each day you have to build a new house, a house that will probably be destroyed that same evening. Even one of our country's most famous ballads is based on the destruction of a newly built castle during the night, every night. So in Albania one must hurry to speak, even at the cost of being harsh and direct. "Do it while you have the chance" are the words we live by. Perhaps this is the secret code of many postcolonial countries that have not been the masters of their own history, places where time means both nothing and everything. Rising from your own ashes like a phoenix and trying to enjoy the fact that you are still alive are our motivation. This basic conflict forms the background of *Child of Nature*. It is there like the faint trace of an old canvas barely visible beneath the new picture painted over it.

So what I've been doing in recent years as my life has partly shifted to America has been nothing less than reconfiguring the relationship between myself and my country, myself and my history, myself and whoever this new self is becoming. I've had to confront all the traps I had tried to escape from in the past: tradition, politics, and sentimentalism. And I think this book is mostly a reflection of this struggle.

Looking over this collection once more, I noticed that the expression "read from the last page" is repeated (silently) in different poems, reminding me that as a child I had the odd habit of starting books from the last page. I don't know how a psychologist would explain it—perhaps merely as impatience or exaggerated curiosity—but in an allegorical way it reveals how my creative process works now: I hurry to a conclusion, then go back and figure out the "why" and "how" of the poetic mechanism. At one point in the poem "Monday in Seven Days," a child breaks apart her toys to reveal their inner mysteries. In this way I suggest that freeing objects of their function is the first step toward understanding them. One could even say that this book is simultaneously a "conclusion" and a "revelation," something that offers the tranquility and tenderness to move closer to objects and discover what is almost impossible to see from a distance: the inner life of things.

Also important during my childhood were the characters that surrounded me. These figures were often tough men, successful at creating epics from a reality in which life was reduced to very little. And so the initial concept of this book was an album of these characters. Creating portraits in mere seconds (that is poetry's nature) was not easy. One person, my uncle Sami, never married and idealized Florence as if he had spent his honeymoon there. It was the only place he had visited outside Albania, and while he was there he got so sick from pneumonia he had to be hospitalized for several months. But to him this trip was the best thing that ever happened in his life. Uncle Sami could be cruel when he constantly shouted at us to "Do your best!" But this was simply his way of balancing the humiliation of the Stalinist regime with an internal pride, while making sure that we were truly alive. It was difficult for a child to understand, so he repeated it systematically—we heard such words more often than we saw food on our table. The men of my family were arrogant, using this to hide their own weaknesses.

"Monday in Seven Days" is set in the small town at the foot of a mountain where I grew up. The summers are dry and small disputes arise because of the perpetual drought; weddings are crowded and unruly—revenge for our miserable lives; deaths echo long and loud through this town where nothing new ever happens. As a child I never heard the word "paradise" or "afterlife" mentioned when someone died, perhaps because the area was once populated by Bektashi Sufis, and according to their beliefs heaven and hell are part of this world. Or perhaps it was because a long prohibition against religious practice simplified the townspeople's concepts of life and death. Death expected nothing more than a sense of respect for the people who would miss the one departed. And then there were those men—dark, shadowy men—who sat in the empty corners of the movie theater just to hide their tears during the saddest parts of the film.

Erotic scandals were a popular topic of conversation in our town. A woman who betrayed her husband was treated much differently from the Madame Bovary we saw on television in the evening. Madame B. was contemptible, yes, but also a movie character, and therefore always an idol. Television news was also frequently discussed, and was always about another place, never fresh, purified by distance, and skimmed over with apathy. Sunday shopping at the peasants' market (the only private market permitted by the government) and the men returning home with fresh green vegetables or an occasional piece of handmade cheese or butter, was always an interesting event, one that had less to do with hunger than with the fact that they had bought something actually produced in one's private garden or home, rather than in a factory or a cooperative.

The calm setting I am describing was interrupted most often by two people: Mustafa, the town drunk, and Zyhra, an abandoned woman. Mustafa was a good target for everybody, a person to make fun of, a tortoise at a funeral or, as I say in one of my poems, a "swab of alcohol-dabbed cotton / pressed to a wound." Zyhra always dressed in rags, rarely stepped out of her house, and was thus a mysterious and intriguing character, especially to children as, in general, the only other mysterious thing we ever saw was a nightmare—the "jeep" that was the secret service car coming to make arrests. There were also the Friday gypsies, women who pretended to read fortunes in threads cut from our clothes in exchange for a piece of bread or cheese, or some oil. Everybody knew they were fakes, but Friday night's sleep was different—magical and hopeful because of their predictions. I also can't forget my neighbor, the madwoman, the one who used to wander the streets and talk in a loud voice to the ghosts of executed ministers or dead politicians. Politics, even in her darkness, was with her everywhere!

There were only a few books on our shelves—the people of our town regarded books with suspicion. The most educated generation of Albanians belonged to the nineteenth century and the beginning of the twentieth, when we were still part of the Ottoman Empire. But when I grew up it was different. It was an era of forbidden books, books that were victims of the cultural revolution, mostly translated Russian classics: Turgenev, Tolstoy, Chekhov, and sometimes an American like Walt Whitman. I never understood why these books were banned, but because of the public library's "circulation conspiracy"—books suddenly disappearing from the shelves—we were obsessed with these titles. When a friend of mine discovered Camus's writings were sequestered in the library's R-sector of blacklisted books, he used all of his connections to see them. But the moment Camus was no longer forbidden, he lost interest in his work.

The end of the Communist regime was followed by a period of rationalization, when people started to question the meanings behind everything. But it seems as if it is even more difficult for Alabanians to write now than ever before, the same way learning to swim is much easier as a child when one has a narrower sense of danger, than when one is an adult and fear becomes greater than the desire to swim. Now, exposed to the wide range of world literature, Albanian writers are suddenly conscious that the water we've been swimming in is much deeper than we had thought.

In the end I think I returned to my initial motivation for writing in *Child of Nature*: simply to record some of the things I saw, heard, and felt, letting the voices of three generations of Albanians who may have thought with loud voices but couldn't speak, filter through. As the saying goes, reveal certain facts and *res ipsa loquitur*, the thing speaks for itself.

LULJETA LLESHANAKU

LULJETA LLESHANAKU was born in Elbasan, Albania in 1968. She grew up under house arrest during Enver Hoxha's Stalinist dictatorship, and so was not permitted to attend college or publish her poetry until the weakening and eventual collapse of the regime in the early 1990s. She eventually studied Albanian philology at the University of Tirana, and has worked as a schoolteacher, literary magazine editor, and journalist. Of her first book, *Fresco: Selected Poetry of Luljeta Lleshanaku*, Robert Creeley wrote, "In this bewildering human world Lleshanaku's articulate determinations prove again our common faith. She speaks to us one and all." HENRY ISRAELI and SHPRESA QATIPI received an NEA Literature Fellowship and a Black Mountain Institute/Rainmakers Grant for the translation of *Child of Nature*.